First World War
and Army of Occupation
War Diary
France, Belgium and Germany

58 DIVISION
Headquarters, Branches and Services
Commander Royal Artillery
13 September 1915 - 29 February 1916

WO95/2992/3

The Naval & Military Press Ltd
www.nmarchive.com
Published in association with The National Archives

Published by

The Naval & Military Press Ltd

Unit 10 Ridgewood Industrial Park,

Uckfield, East Sussex,

TN22 5QE England

Tel: +44 (0) 1825 749494

www.naval-military-press.com

www.nmarchive.com

This diary has been reprinted in facsimile from the original. Any imperfections are inevitably reproduced and the quality may fall short of modern type and cartographic standards.

© Crown Copyright
Images reproduced by permission of The National Archives, London, England, 2015.

Contents

Document type	Place/Title	Date From	Date To
Heading	WO95/2992/3		
Heading	58 Division (2/1 London Div) C.R.A 1915 Sep-1916 Feb		
Miscellaneous	Statement By C.R.A. 58th (London) Divisional Artillery	02/09/1915	02/09/1915
War Diary	Warren Heath Camp	13/09/1915	13/09/1915
War Diary	Saxmundham (Hurts Hall Park)	13/09/1915	13/09/1915
War Diary	Framlingham	13/09/1915	13/09/1915
War Diary	Warren Heath Camp	13/09/1915	13/09/1915
War Diary	Sidegate Lane Camp	13/09/1915	13/09/1915
War Diary	Warren Heath Camp	20/09/1915	20/09/1915
War Diary	Saxmundham (Hurts Hall Park)	20/09/1915	20/09/1915
War Diary	Warren Heath Camp	20/09/1915	20/09/1915
War Diary	Framlingham	20/09/1915	20/09/1915
War Diary	Kettering	20/09/1915	20/09/1915
War Diary	Tadworth	20/09/1915	20/09/1915
War Diary	Warren Heath Camp	24/09/1915	24/09/1915
War Diary	Sidegate Lane Camp	24/09/1915	24/09/1915
War Diary	Warren Heath Camp	25/09/1915	25/09/1915
War Diary	Saxmundham (Hurts Hall Park)	25/09/1915	25/09/1915
War Diary	Framlingham	25/09/1915	25/09/1915
War Diary	Red House Park	25/09/1915	25/09/1915
War Diary	Warren Heath Camp	27/09/1915	27/09/1915
War Diary	Bury St Edmunds	30/09/1915	30/09/1915
War Diary	Redhouse Ipswich	13/10/1915	13/10/1915
War Diary	Red House Park Ipswich	30/11/1915	30/11/1915
War Diary	Martlesham Heath	07/12/1915	07/12/1915
War Diary	Priory Heath	10/12/1915	11/12/1915
War Diary	Brightwell Heath	13/12/1915	13/12/1915
War Diary	Framlingham	14/12/1915	14/12/1915
War Diary	Martlesham Heath	28/12/1915	28/12/1915
War Diary	Ipswich	13/01/1916	13/01/1916
War Diary	Orford	19/01/1916	23/02/1916
War Diary	Ipswich	29/02/1916	29/02/1916

WO 95/2992/3

58 DIVISION (2/1 LONDON DIV)

C.R.A.

1915 SEP — 1916 FEB

Confidential

Statement by C.R.A., 58th (London) Divisional Artillery.

Division.	58th (London) Division.
Mobilization Centre.	London.
Temporary War Station.	Full details given in October statement.
Concentration at War Station.	No further remarks.

Organization for Defence.   Since the last statement was rendered a large number of Remounts have been received. These are now being given slow work.

New G.S. harness has also been supplied.

All Units are now in a position to move all their equipment in the event of a sudden move.

Training.   Good progress is being made by all Units.

The personnel are fit for active service.

Field telephones are required.

Arrangements are being made for the 25% of the 2nd Line Units attached for training to rejoin their own Brigades about the 9th September. Further drafts are being sent to replace them.

4 howitzer guns are on loan to the 1 "B" Reserve Brigade R.F.A. at Ipswich Barracks. This hampers to some extent the training of the 1/4th London (Howitzer) Brigade and the 2nd Line men attached to this Brigade for instruction.

One Field Battery is still at Kettering and one at Richmond Park. Both these Batteries are being used for instructional purposes.

Two guns of the 1/1st London Brigade R.F.A. sent to Woolwich for repair have not been returned.

Discipline.   Satisfactory.

Administration.   No further remarks.

Supply of Remounts.   A large number of Remounts have been received during the month.

These are mostly Canadian horses and are of a satisfactory type.

Organization into Home & Imperial Service.   All ranks are for Imperial Service.

Red House Park,
Ipswich,
2.9.15.

F. Seaver.
Colonel,
Commanding Artillery,
58th (London) Division.

Sheet 1

Headquarters
58th London Original Artillery
Athenia Park
Warwick

Army Form C. 2118.

SECRET.

WAR DIARY

INTELLIGENCE SUMMARY.

(Erase heading not required.)

Instructions regarding War Diaries and Intelligence Summaries are contained in F.S. Regs., Part II. and the Staff Manual respectively. Title pages will be prepared in manuscript.

Hour, Date, Place	Summary of Events and Information	Remarks and references to Appendices
13th September 1915 WARREN HEATH CAMP	A draft of 5 Officers 143 other ranks from the 2/1st London Brigade R.F.A. from Bloomsbury joined at Warren Heath for training with the 1/1st London Brigade R.F.A.	C in C
13th September 1915 SAXMUNDHAM (North Hall Park)	A draft of 3 Officers 150 other ranks from the 4/2nd London Brigade R.F.A. from Woolwich arrived at Saxmundham for training with the 1/2nd London Brigade R.F.A.	C in C
13th September 1915 FRAMLINGHAM	A draft of 7 Officers 149 other ranks from the 2/3rd London Brigade R.F.A. from Tournay Street, City arrived at Framlingham for training with the 1/3rd London Brigade R.F.A.	C in C
13th September 1915 WARREN HEATH CAMP	A draft of 3 Officers 94 other ranks from the 4/4th London (How) Brigade R.F.A. from Ennersdale Road Lewisham S.E. arrived at Warren Heath for training with the 1/4th London (How) Brigade for R.G.A. Two Officers 30 N.C.O.s and men from the 2nd Line from London to be attached for training to the 1/1st London Heavy Battery R.G.A.	C in C
13th September 1915 VIDEGATE LANE CAMP		C in C

Sheet II

Secret.

Army Form C. 2118.

WAR DIARY

INTELLIGENCE SUMMARY.

(Erase heading not required.)

Instructions regarding War Diaries and Intelligence Summaries are contained in F. S. Regs., Part II. and the Staff Manual respectively. Title pages will be prepared in manuscript.

Hour, Date, Place	Summary of Events and Information	Remarks and references to Appendices
20th September 1915 WARREN HEATH CAMP	An advance party consisting of 3 Officers 100 other ranks of the 2/11th London Brigade R.F.A. arrived at Warren Heath to take over the equipment, stores etc of the 1/11th London Brigade R.F.A. proceeding overseas.	G.S.L
20th September 1915 SAX MUNDHAM (Hurts Hall Park)	An advance party consisting of 3 Officers 100 other ranks of the 2/12th London Brigade R.F.A. arrived at Saxmundham to take over the equipment, stores etc. of the 1/12th London Brigade R.F.A. proceeding overseas.	G.S.L
20th September 1915 WARREN HEATH CAMP	An advance party consisting of 3 Officers 100 other ranks of the 2/14th London (Hows) Brigade R.F.A. arrived at Warren Heath to take over the equipment, stores etc. of the 1/4th London (Hows) Brigade R.F.A. proceeding overseas.	G.S.L
20th September 1915 FRAMLINGHAM	An advance party consisting of 3 Officers 100 other ranks of the 2/13th London Brigade R.F.A. arrived at Framlingham to take over the equipment, stores etc. of the 1/13th London Brigade R.F.A. proceeding overseas.	G.S.L

Sheet III Sheet.

Army Form C. 2118

WAR DIARY
INTELLIGENCE SUMMARY
(Erase heading not required.)

Instructions regarding War Diaries and Intelligence Summaries are contained in F. S. Regs., Part II. and the Staff Manual respectively. Title Pages will be prepared in manuscript.

Place	Date	Hour	Summary of Events and Information	Remarks and references to Appendices
KETTERING	19/9/16		1 Officer and 15 other ranks from the 2/1st London Brigade R.F.A. took over the horses and equipment left by the 2/2nd London Batty R.F.A. at the Artillery Training Centre at Kettering.	Gi. RFA
TADWORTH	20/9/16		1 Officer and 15 other ranks from the 2/6th Battery R.F.A. took over the horses, equipment and guns from the 2/6th Battery R.F.A. at Tadworth.	Gi. RFA
WARREN HEATH CAMP	24/9/16		8 Officers 148 other ranks, 84 horses from the 2/4th London (How) Brigade R.F.A. arrived at Warren Heath.	Gi. RFA
MOE GATE – LANE CAMP	24/9/16		3 Officers, 171 other ranks, 40 horses from the 2/1st London Battery R.G.A. arrived at Lidgate Lane.	Gi. RGA
WARREN HEATH CAMP	27/9/16		16 Officers, 366 other ranks, 115 horses from the 2/1st London Brigade R.F.A. arrived at Warren Heath.	Gi. RFA
SAXMUNDHAM (Saint Batty Pk)	27/9/16		5 Officers, 130 other ranks from the 2/22nd London Brigade R.G.A. arrived at Saxmundham.	Gi. RFA
FRAMLINGHAM	27/9/16		13 Officers 343 other ranks 117 horses from the 2/3rd London Brigade R.F.A. arrived at Framlingham.	Gi. RFA
GEO. HOUSE PARK	29/9/16		1 Officer, 3 other ranks from Headquarters (2/1st London Gri. Artillery) Indian Home arrived in Ipswich.	Gri. Gi. RFA

Vol. IV Sheet 1.

WAR DIARY
INTELLIGENCE SUMMARY

Army Form C. 2118

Place	Date	Hour	Summary of Events and Information	Remarks and references to Appendices
WARREN HEATH CAMP	27/9/15		1 Officer & 19 other ranks of the 2/1st London Bgde R.F.A. arrived at Warren Heath.	G.S.S.
BURY ST EDMUNDS	30/9/15		5 horses taken over from the first lived by the 2/4th London H.S. (How.) Brigade R.F.A. were sent to the Veterinary Hospital at Bury St Edmunds.	G.S.S.

C. J. Sheffield
Adjutant
2/II London Divisional Artillery
4 Oct 1915

WAR DIARY
or
INTELLIGENCE SUMMARY.

Army Form C. 2118.

(Erase heading not required.)

Instructions regarding War Diaries and Intelligence Summaries are contained in F.S. Regs., Part II. and the Staff Manual respectively. Title pages will be prepared in manuscript.

Place	Date	Hour	Summary of Events and Information	Remarks and references to Appendices
Redhouse Pk. IPSWICH	13/10/15		Captain P. Bayldon, 2/2nd London Brigade R.F.A. arrived to take up duties of A/Staff Captain, at these Headquarters.	

E.J.Griffith Capt RA
for Colonel,
Commanding Artillery,
58th London Division.
2/11/15

Army Form C. 2118.

WAR DIARY
~~INTELLIGENCE SUMMARY~~
(Erase heading not required.)

Instructions regarding War Diaries and Intelligence Summaries are contained in F. S. Regs., Part II. and the Staff Manual respectively. Title pages will be prepared in manuscript.

Place	Date	Hour	Summary of Events and Information	Remarks and references to Appendices
Redhouse Park IPSWICH	30.11.15		NIL	

[Stamp: 58th (LONDON) DIVISION GENERAL STAFF 3 — DEC. 1915]

F. Newel.
Colonel,
Commanding Artillery,
58th London Division.

Army Form C. 2118

WAR DIARY
or
~~INTELLIGENCE SUMMARY~~
(Erase heading not required.)

Instructions regarding War Diaries and Intelligence Summaries are contained in F.S. Regs., Part II. and the Staff Manual respectively. Title Pages will be prepared in manuscript.

58th (LONDON) DIVISION
4 - JAN. 1916
GENERAL STAFF

Place	Date	Hour	Summary of Events and Information	Remarks and references to Appendices
Martlesham Heath.	Dec. 7th.		2/1st, 2/2nd and 2/4th London Brigades R.F.A. Inspected by Lieut. General Broadwood, G.O.C. 1st. Army.	
Priory Heath	Dec. 10th.		2/1st London Brigade R.F.A. Inspected by Major General Brunker, Inspector of R.H. and R.F.A.	
Priory Heath	Dec. 11th		2/4th London Brigade R.F.A. Inspected by Major General Brunker, Inspector of R.H. and R.F.A.	
Brightwell Heath.	Dec. 13th		2/2nd London Brigade R.F.A. Inspected by Major General Brunker, Inspector of R.H. & R.F.A.	
Framlingham	Dec. 14th		2/3rd London Brigade R.F.A. Inspected by Major General Brunker, Inspector of R.H. & R.F.A.	
Martlesham Heath	Dec. 28th		2/1st 2/2nd and 2/4th London Brigades R.F.A. Inspected by Brig. Gen. E.J. Cooper, G.O.C. 58th (London) Division.	

Rednouse Park,
Ipswich,
4.1.1916.

E.J.Griffiths Capt R.A.
for Colonel,
Commanding Artillery,
58th (London) Division.

Army Form C. 2118.

WAR DIARY
INTELLIGENCE SUMMARY *58th London Divisional Artillery*

(Erase heading not required.)

Place	Date	Hour	Summary of Events and Information	Remarks and references to Appendices
IPSWICH.	13.1.16.		Brigadier General E.J.Granet C.B. assumed Command of 58th London Divisional Artillery vice Colonel F.Beaver.	X
ORFORD	19.1.16.		2/4th London Battery,R.F.A. Instructional Firing Practice. ORFORD-ALDEBURGH RANGE	
	20.1.16.		2/3rd " " " " " "	
	21.1.16.		2/1st " " " " " "	
	22.1.16.		2/2nd " " " " " "	
	24.1.16.		2/7th " " " " " "	
	25.1.16.		2/8th " " " " " " 2	
	26.1.16.		2/9th " " " " " "	
	27.1.16.		2/5th " " " " " "	
	28.1.16.		2/6th " " " " " "	
	29.1.16.		2/4th " " " " " "	

Redhouse Park,
Ipswich
2.2.16.

E.J. Granet
Brig.Gen.
Commanding Artillery,
58th London Division.

58th Division Artillery

Army Form C. 2118.

WAR DIARY
INTELLIGENCE SUMMARY.
(Erase heading not required.)

Instructions regarding War Diaries and Intelligence Summaries are contained in F.S. Regs., Part II. and the Staff Manual respectively. Title pages will be prepared in manuscript.

Place	Date	Hour	Summary of Events and Information	Remarks and references to Appendices
ORFORD	23.2.16		Firing practice (Officers), carried out by 2/10 Battery 2/4 Howitzer Brigade on the ORFORD ALDBURGH RANGE with 15 pr. guns.	
Ipswich	24.2.16		Major A.K.G. WHITE R.F.A took over duties of Brigade Major	

Willett Brigade Major
for Brig. Gen.
Commanding Artillery
58th London Division

Ipswich
3.3.16